Ants

by **Trudi Strain Trueit**

Reading Consultant: Nanci R. Vargus, Ed.D.

Marshall Cavendish
Benchmark
New York

Picture Words

 ants

 caterpillars

 flowers

 ladybugs

 leaves

 seeds

 sticks

are small, but strong.

🐜🐜🐜 can lift 🌰🌰.

can lift .

can lift .

 can lift .

can lift

other .

14

can lift .

can lift

cannot lift you!

Words to Know

lift
    to carry or move

strong (strawng)
    having power; not weak

Find Out More

Books

Birch, Robin. *Ants Up Close*. Chicago, IL: Raintree, 2004.

Lockwood, Sophie. *Ants*. Mankato, MN: Child's World, 2007.

Parker, Steve. *Ant Lions, Wasps and Other Insects*. Minneapolis, MN: Compass Point Books, 2005.

Schulte, Mary. *Ants and Other Insects*. New York: Children's Press, 2005.

DVDs

Insects. TMW Media Group, 2008.

NOVA: Ants! Little Creatures Who Run the World. WGBH, Boston, 2007.

Web Sites

Natural History Museum: Antcam
www.nhm.ac.uk/kids-only/naturecams/antcam/index.html

PBS Kids: Backyard Jungle
www.pbskids.org/backyardjungle

About the Author

Trudi Strain Trueit has written more than forty nonfiction books for children, from early readers to biographies to self-help books for teens. She writes fiction, too, and is the author of the popular *Julep O'Toole* series for middle-grade readers. Born and raised in the Pacific Northwest, Trudi lives near Seattle, Washington, with her husband. She has a B.A. in broadcast journalism. Learn more about Trudi and her books at **www.truditrueit.com**.

About the Reading Consultant

Nanci R. Vargus, Ed.D., used to teach first grade. Now she works at the University of Indianapolis. Nanci helps young people become teachers. Her first graders enjoyed watching the busy ants in the class ant farm.

Marshall Cavendish Benchmark
99 White Plains Road
Tarrytown, NY 10591-5502
www.marshallcavendish.us

All Internet addresses were correct at the time of printing.

Library of Congress Cataloging-In-Publication Data
Trueit, Trudi Strain.
Ants / by Trudi Strain Trueit.
    p. cm. — (Benchmark rebus. Creepy critters)
Includes bibliographical references.
Summary: "Easy to read text with rebuses explores the strength of the ant"—Provided by publisher.
ISBN 978-0-7614-3961-5
1. Ants—Juvenile literature. I. Title.
QL568.F7T57 2009
595.79'6—dc22
        2008012152

Editor: Christine Florie
Publisher: Michelle Bisson
Art Director: Anahid Hamparian
Series Designer: Virginia Pope

Photo research by Connie Gardner

Rebus images provided courtesy of *Dorling Kindersley.*

Cover photo by James Robinson/Animals, Animals

The photographs in this book are used with permission and through the courtesy of:
Superstock: p. 5 age footstock; *Getty Images*: p. 9 Tom Flack; p. 11 Gail Shumway; p. 15 Mark Moffett; *Minden Pictures*: pp. 7, 13 Mark Moffett; *Corbis*: p. 17 Klaus Hana; p. 21 Jon Feingersh; *Peter Anrold*: p. 19 J. Kottman.

Printed in Malaysia
1 3 5 6 4 2